Rug Hooking

Table of content

Part 1 7

Chapter One: A Brief History of Rug Hooking 7

Chapter Two: How to Hook 11

    Having the Right Tools 11

    Choice of Fabrics 11

    The Ideal Yarn 12

    The Frame 12

    Finding Balance 12

    Troubleshooting 12

Chapter Three: How to Hook 14

    Rug Hook Genres 14

        Hoop or Frame 15

        Backing 15

        Wool 15

        Cutter 15

        Virgin Wool 17

        Worsted Wool 17

        Merino Wool 18

Tweeds 19

Best weight for rug hooking 19

Wool Labeling 20

Primitive Style 20

Realistic Style 21

Pictorial Style 21

Abstract or Geometric Style 21

Waldoboro Style 22

Chapter Four: How to Draw a Pattern 23

Burlap 23

Rug Warp 25

Chapter Five: Finishing a Hooked Rug 26

Chapter Six: Care, Storage and Cleaning 31

Storage 31

Care 31

Cleaning 33

Part Two 35

Making a Latch Hook Pillow 35

Making a Latch Hook Wall Hanging 36

Making Latch Hooking Coasters 38

Conclusion 42

© **Copyright 2018 - All rights reserved.**

The contents of this book may not be reproduced, duplicated or transmitted without direct written permission from the author.

Under no circumstances will any legal responsibility or blame be held against the publisher for any reparation, damages, or monetary loss due to the information herein, either directly or indirectly.

Legal Notice:

This book is copyright protected. This is only for personal use. You cannot amend, distribute, sell, use, quote or paraphrase any part or the content within this book without the consent of the author.

Disclaimer Notice:

Please note the information contained within this document is for educational and entertainment purposes only. Every attempt has been made to provide accurate, up to date and complete, reliable information. No warranties of any kind are expressed or implied. Readers acknowledge that the author is not engaging in the rendering of legal, financial, medical or professional advice. The content of this book has been derived from various sources. Please consult a licensed professional before attempting any techniques outlined in this book.

By reading this document, the reader agrees that under no circumstances are the author responsible for any losses, direct or indirect, which are incurred as a result of the use of information contained within this document, including, but not limited to, —errors, omissions, or inaccuracies.

Introduction

Rug hooking is a unique and creative way to detail patterns during rug making. They can not only be laid on the floor but also hung on the wall like paintings. There is no agreement as to the origin of the technique.

Part 1

Chapter One: A Brief History of Rug Hooking

Rug hooking is a craft that has existed for centuries. The exact origin is up for debate by historians, but the earliest accounts date back to between the third and seventh centuries. Descendants of the early Egyptians were thought to have made the first hand-hooked rugs, but alternative theories stated that it was the Chinese.

Another theory espoused by the author, William Winthrop Kent says that rug hooking began in England. In the early part of the nineteenth-century floor mats in England were hooked rugs. Weaving mill workers collected thrums, which were pieces of yarn smaller than nine inches in length as they were useless to the mill. They would then pull them through the backing material to make a rug.

Jenni Stuart Anderson, another author, believed that the Vikings brought rug hooking to Scotland. They used the technique to hook woolen loops through a backing fabric. Relics of this art remain at Fold Museum in Guernsey, Channel Islands. Other examples of rug hooking have been traced to the coast of France and Egypt as well.

The modern version of rug hooking, however, originated along the Eastern Seaboard of the United States, in New England. It has also been traced to the Canadian Maritimes, Newfoundland, and Labrador from the mid-nineteenth century. Hook rugs began as an alternative for those who couldn't afford to import carpets from England. In a primitive version of recycling, weavers used any spare scraps of cloth they could find for lack of better alternatives. This usually consisted of burlap from sacks since cotton was too expensive to waste. After 1849, when the British Acts of Trade were repealed and the technology needed to produce cotton became cheaper, the trade developed both technologically and creatively. As demand for hooked rugs grew, it became more profitable to produce them; if time-consuming. Edward Sands Frost conceived the idea of using stencils made from old copper boilers to print designs in the 1870s. The hook rugs became trendy however in the 20th century; the quality of rugs diminished significantly and demand was replaced by machine-made carpets.

Rug hooking was saved from extinction by two people; Pearl McGown and William Winthrop Kent. Pearl taught the art to others and thus kept it alive while Kent published three books promoting the craft and encouraging readers to weave new rugs. The craft not only gained popularity in the US but Europe as well, especially Denmark. A Danish citizen named Ernst Thomsen invented a rug hooking machine in 1939, which used yarn. This led to increased production, which enabled the rugs to gain even more popularity. After the Second World War, with the help of his daughter, Jane, and her husband, Kare, he went into industrial manufacture and design of the rugs. They sold the company in 1987 to Sussi

Lunden who still supplies equipment and materials to rug hookers.

Chapter Two: How to Hook

Now that we know about the where rug hooking came from, we're going to take a look at how to go about making a rug using this method. We'll begin with a few tips to get a rug hooker started.

Having the Right Tools

Like any other craft, many different styles of tools are associated with rug hooking. This includes the Amy Oxford needle, which is highly prized, vintage model rug hookers or rug prodders. They all work by forming continuous loops using hooking yarn fed through the backing fabric.

Choice of Fabrics

The base of the rug is formed by foundation fabric and therefore it is important to choose a backing fabric that is strong, durable, has sufficiently loose weave to let the wool through and is cost-efficient.

The Ideal Yarn

The most durable yarn is a three-ply wool rug yarn. Chunky yarns are effective, but the smaller weighted yarns can be doubled up to thicken them.

The Frame

As a novice, it is best to begin with an embroidery hoop to hold the backing fabric in place. As your confidence and skills grow, it will be necessary to get a wooden frame from which you can create larger projects like rugs or cushions. You stretch the backing fabric taut enough on the frame to bounce a coin off of. If the coin doesn't bounce, you need to tighten the stretch.

Finding Balance

You may not achieve a balance between your needle, fabric, and yarn right away. It takes a few tries to get it right. Be prepared to experiment with different loop sizes, backing materials and hooks. Start slowly but keep the pace constant.

Troubleshooting

If the loops are not forming correctly, you may need to check that your yarn isn't caught on anything. There should be a free flow between the yarn and the needle and if there isn't, it means there is some sort of blockage that you need to resolve to have a trouble free rug hooking session.

Chapter Three: How to Hook

Rug Hook Genres

New materials and techniques to rug hook have been discovered in recent decades. Two main genres have emerged.

The first one is *Fine Hooking* in which strips of wool measuring 1/32" to 5/32" are used. The shading used in fine-cut hooking is finer, and the designs use over dyed wool in graduated color swatches.

The second one is primitive or wide-cut hooking, which uses strips of wool with a width of between 6/32" and 1/2". This type of rug hooking uses the texture of wools, such as herringbones, plaids, and checks to achieve highlighting and shading. They are generally less detailed resembling earlier designs of rug hooking.

There are certain basic tools that are used for rug hooking.

Hoop or Frame

An embroidery or quilting hoop or frame is used. Novices start out with hooks before graduating to frames specifically designed for the task. Some hooks have special handles which assist people with physically compromised people to still craft the rugs such as those with arthritis.

Backing

The woolen strips must be hooked into a backing material which can be made of monk's cloth, burlap, linen or rug warp. Anything made of porous material that would allow the hook to pull the wool strip through the backing.

Wool

Wool is an easily available material that can be obtained from thrift stores, a haberdashery or on a website which is then cut into strips. Yardage can also be used.

Cutter

It is possible to cut wool by hand by sniping one inch or less from the edge and then ripping the rest. A small bladed pair of scissors can be used to cut it in half and then each half into half again. That produces strips of about a quarter inch.

A rotary cutter can also be used due to the spongy texture of wool, which makes it more difficult to cut than cotton. If the rug hooker is using scissors, a small bladed one works better. If possible, the wool is ripped to keep it on the straight of grain. A wool cutter or stripper will produce three-inch-wide strips before they run through the cutter.

Types of Rug Hooking Wool

Wool is a generic term used to refer to the fleece of many domesticated animals from sheep to llamas. Each of these species has different breeds, which serve different purposes; some are bred for food, others for their fleece, while some serve a dual purpose. In addition to these two major reasons, other domesticated animals simply serve as pets, or for transportation and pack animals. Some of this wool is better suited to rug hooking than others.

Virgin Wool

This type of wool refers to the kind that has never been used for any other purpose. It is new and not repurposed from other garments or uses. The fabric that comes from repurposed wool is known as 'shoddy' and this is why the term infers low quality. Repurposed wool is not really suitable for rug hooking, but virgin wool is.

Worsted Wool

This is the type of cloth made from long staple wool like Merino and has a more concentrated twist. The fibers are perfectly aligned with a smooth surface. The weave used on it is usually twill. Worsted wool is not suitable for hooking because they easily unravel. This is because of the smooth surface, which means there are no interlocking hairs when pulled.

Pendleton Wool

This is a good wool for hooking, manufactured in the US. In addition, the Pendleton flannel wool, which is a weave, made using woolen yarn and brushed finish, is also good for hooking.

Houndstooth

This type of wool is woven into fabric resulting in a distinct checked pattern made up of two colors, which interlock.

Herringbone

This type of fabric is woven using a warp and a weft in different colors, and twill weave forming an interlocking V pattern of stripes.

Cashmere Wool

This highly prized wool is obtained from a goat species called Cashmere and is popular due to its soft light feel. It is a good wool for hooking.

Merino Wool

Merino sheep have long fleece that is fine yet thick. This fleece is used to make worsted wool as the long staple fibers. This means the finished product has fewer hairs on the finished surface. It's a good candidate for hooking.

Tweeds

This is a heavy cloth originating from the border of England and Scotland along the banks of River Tweed. It is manufactured using a very special yarn garnered from the wool of Cheviot and Herwick sheep, which have very rough fleece. The fabric is usually woven from Marled or Heathered yarn using many muted colors spun together into a plaid, check or stripe pattern with a herringbone weave. It is a warm hairy or brushed cloth and can be fine and fashionable or rough and durable.

Best weight for rug hooking

The size of the strips is dependent on the weight of the wool fabric used. In spite of the fabric used, a minimum of four or five threads are needed in order for the strip to hold together while hooking. A wider cut is suitable for lightweight fabric, but they will collapse if hooked in thicker sizes. Two strips might work better because the thinner sizes will not stand erect or neatly. Fraying heavy fabric will enable them to be used for finer detail hooking.

Wool Labeling

Wool mills are licensed to use a Wool Mark which indicates that their product is pure new wool and of high quality. This mark is internationally recognized and resembles a shamrock with interlacing lines. However, having the Wool Mark does not guarantee that the fabric is suitable for rug hooking.

There are different styles to rug hooking. The advantage rug hooking is that there is not much time investment put into learning different skills or stitches. There is just one basic stitch and once it is mastered that is all that's needed. There are different styles of stitching, however. These include:

Primitive Style

This is the easiest style to master for novices. Wide strips of wool of about a quarter inch wide are used to outline a simple design. There is no need for realism in style or color and one can even use a children's book to obtain designs from.

Children's coloring books are chock full of simple designs that can be used to make a pattern or you can make your own.

Realistic Style

The strip of wool used in this type of rug is narrower with a width of three twenty-thirds to one-eighth of an inch. The aim is to add as much detail as possible and make the design realistic. Several shades of each color are used, and this is achieved by dying white wool to the exact target shade. This gives the rug a very lively appearance.

Pictorial Style

The rug hooker creates a picture or landscape then uses the wool to bring it to life. The width used may vary from all wide to all narrow to an assortment of both. The creator uses the hooks to bring the picture to life.

Abstract or Geometric Style

This style is made up of circles, squares, diamonds, triangles and other geometric designs. It is another design that is suitable for novices. The width of the wool can vary.

Waldoboro Style

This style got it's moniker from the town of Waldoboro Maine because the women their innovated their own rug hooking style. It is distinct in two ways. The first is that wool backing is used for rug hooking rather than burlap, linen or monk's cloth. The second is that following hooking of the design; the wool is trimmed and shaped to create a three-dimensional shape.

Chapter Four: How to Draw a Pattern

A pattern on the backing can either be purchased from a store or the rug hooker can create their own. This is done by drawing a pattern on a paper. You can experiment with various copies having different color palettes. The drawing can be expanded to fit the backing. A red dot, which is a thin and see-through fabric with interfacings and has a red dot on every inch, can be used. This red dot is placed over the paper pattern, which is then traced over with a pen or pencil. The red dot is placed in the center of the backing and traced with a fabric pen.

The base of the rug can be made of various materials. These include:

Burlap

Burlap is not considered to be as strong as linen or rug warp, but it is the most inexpensive backing. However, most rug hookers don't like to use it because it's longevity of use is not as strong. The weave on burlap is also very uneven and it is an abrasive surface to work on.

Burlap comes in many types, including feedbags, which are what early rug hookers used. It has a finer weave than most burlap currently used.

Monk's Cloth

Most novices will come across monk's cloth when just starting out since it is the material that most commercial patterns are drawn on. It is identified by the white fibers that run across the fabric and the double weave of the cloth. This feature makes it easy to catch the loops when the rug hooker pulls it through, and that is why it is a favorite with novices. Monk's cloth causes difficulty when trying to pull a wide cut if the hooker inserts the hook between the fibers. The backing tends to get overstretched leading to over-hooking at that particular spot. The result of this is that the rug does not lie straight but tends to curl.

Rug Warp

It is made of pure cotton and produces a very even weave, which means the rugs stay flat. The outer edge is easy to hook and transfer of patterns or drawing on them takes place more smoothly since the hooker can follow a straight, flat edge.

Linen

this type of backing is the most expensive and not nearly as soft as pure cotton. The weave is slightly uneven and so hooking in a straight line is not as easy as with cotton.

Chapter Five: Finishing a Hooked Rug

Once you finish hooking the rug, the next step is to make it suitable for its designated uses. The hooked rug can be used as wall tapestry as art, made into a pillow, or laid on the floor to act as a rug. It can also be sewn into a backing to make a bag. These are just some ideas of what to do with a hooked rug, but the list is not exhaustive. There is also an endless number of ways that the rug can be finished.

As soon as you finish hooking, the next step is to turn the mat over to the back and examine it carefully for loose loops and gaps in the burlap that may need an extra loop or more. It is also important to find any tails left behind. If all is in order, the next step is to press the mat.

A moderately damp cloth and extremely hot iron are used to press the mat, along its backside. In order to avoid pressing areas that are meant to be textured, care must be taken when pressing not to flatten them. Pressing can also be done from the front and the pressing cloth is wetted if necessary.

A simple hem using whip stitch is one way to finish a hooked rug. The extra burlap is trimmed, maintaining a distance of one and a half inches away from the actual hooking. This is done by turning the burlap back a quarter inch and then reversing it right up to the hooking line. Upholstery or quilting thread with a very strong needle whip stitch is used with matched backing to turn the back of the hooking and ensure that the hooks are sewn into the backing and not just the loops.

Once you have sewn all four sides, you can press the rug again on the backside, with a focus on the edges. This is an efficient method if the piece is small enough to be hung up with two pins or in a frame to be hung on the wall.

A rug can also be finished is by taking the above steps and then taping the back of the mat with a one and a half inch wide strip of webbed cotton to cover the hemmed over edge. Both sides of the binding tape must be hand sewn. Mats that are finished like this are usually meant to be put on the floor. The binding tape is used to stop the burlap backing from wearing. This type of finish can also be used when the rug is meant to be a chair pad.

A bigger or heavier rug, which is meant to be hung for long periods of time, should utilize an inexpensive curtain rod together with a binding tape sleeve along the top. This holds the weight of the rug evenly and prevents sagging over time. A rug can also be finished using binding tape that is visible on both front and back, rolling the excess burlap inside of the tape.

A whipped edge finish can either match or contrast the rug and it is another way to finish a mat. It is sometimes used to frame the design or it can just be used as a finish that merges with the background or complements the design. To use this finishing method, a quarter inch cotton cord is used together with binding tape, a needle, thread, and yarn. After pressing and trimming the excess burlap, hold a cotton cord strand against the back of the mat using the cord edge against the edge of the last row of a hooked rug. The burlap is folded over the cord, covering it toward the back of the mat.

A strong needle and thread are used to sew a running stitch to the burlap, fusing the layers together with the cord in between. It is essential that the cord is not buckling or stretched too tight. The stitching goes all around the rug before trimming the cord at the beginning point without overlapping the cord. The thread is knotted before the whipping begins by replacing thread with wool yarn. The loose ends of the wool are carefully tucked in together with the cord between the burlap layers. The needle is pushed up, either in front or back, with wool through the holes in the burlap. The wool is pulled up snug before a whip stitch is used to wrap it all up, making sure no burlap is showing and the yarn is lying side by side. As many joins as necessary are made as you stitch all the way around.

Once that task is completed the binding tape is sewn to the back of the mat.

Chapter Six: Care, Storage and Cleaning

Storage

Hooked rugs should never be folded. Instead, they should be rolled lightly, pile side out so as not to damage the burlap backing. No textile should be wrapped in plastic since the resulting trapped moisture will cause mildew. Instead, a clean white cotton towel, sheet or pillowcase should be used, tied loosely. Do not store hooked rugs in cool, damp places prone to mildew and mold or rooms where the temperatures go to extremes like an attic.

Care

When on the floor, the hooked rug should be cared for in the following ways;

- It should be away from high traffic areas prone to wetness like bathrooms, kitchens or doorways.
- A non-sticky, thin, high-quality rug pad needs to be used. It should be a half inch smaller than the hook rug

on all sides with frequent inspections done to avoid wear.

- The yarn which has been hand dyed will be prone to fading if exposed to bright sunlight. Location of the rug should take this into account.
- Do not coat the hand hooked rugs with any chemicals, latex or scotch guard.
- Backing or underlining the hook rug with fabric is a bad idea because it causes dirt and grit to be trapped in between the pile and foundation, which leads to the destruction of the fibers.

A hanging hooked rug should be cared for by:

- Even distribution of the weight of the textile by hanging it from a dowel. The dowel should be inserted through a hand sewn, hand woven, non-stretch fabric made of cotton or linen. The sleeve should be stitched to the back top surface of the rug.
- Tape, glue or adhesive should be avoided.
- Professionally prepared, museum quality, acid-free frames should be used and air permeable backing must

be added if the frame is kept under glass to avoid trapping moisture in the material.

- Wood is a source of discoloration and acid and must not be allowed in direct contact with the rug.

Cleaning

To clean and maintain a hooked rug, always remember that vacuuming too vigorously or added wetness is ill-advised as are house pets. A gentle, hand-held vacuum should be used for cleaning. You can also use a cheesecloth covered upholstery or floor attachment to reduce the suction force. A hooked rug should never be immersed in water to be washed because once the backing is saturated with water, the wool pile will prevent complete drying that will lead to mold, mildew, and rot.

As soon as a stain occurs, it should be blotted with a white cloth and you should never use harsh chemicals or detergents. Using a dry cleaner or cleaning company is ill-advised as they may not handle the rug properly.

Occasionally turn the rug over to remove sand and dirt but don't beat or hang it from a clothesline. You can lay it on a clean piece of paper upside down in order to expose it to sunlight. Hooked rugs should be taken to a restorer for repair at the first sign of wear.

Part Two
Making a Latch Hook Pillow

A latch hook pillow can be fashioned from a hooked rug, created using a small-sized hooked rug. It can enhance the décor of any room with its soft downy uplifting feel. It is not necessary to use a sewing machine to make the pillow. However several other tools are needed. This includes:

- Measuring tape
- Scissors
- Pins
- A latch hook piece
- Heavy fabric
- An iron
- Stuffing
- Heavy thread

Once the hooking process is completed, the first step in converting it into a pillow is to trim the extra burlap, leaving three rows empty. Measure the length and width of the hooked piece and then add four inches to each side, which is the same as the measurement for the backing fabric. The latter is ironed flat to three-quarter of an inch to the edge of the hooked piece and then folded beneath the empty canvas that runs along the hooked rug edges.

The next step is to place the backing and the pillow against each other, right sides together and pin them before sewing the pieces by hand. A heavy thread is used to ensure the strength of the bond. As it is sewn, any extra fullness gets smoothed out all the way around except for an eight-inch allowance on one side, for the purpose of turning the pillow inside out for stuffing. After that is completed, the opening is stitched shut.

Making a Latch Hook Wall Hanging

The first step is to make a design plan by collecting the yarn and choosing the colors.

Next step is to create a blank canvas using any photo editing program to create patterns in the yarn colors selected. One such program is Photoshop Elements, but even simple Microsoft programs like Paint can do the trick. You can also draw by hand, trying out different styles and patterns until you find a design that you're happy with. There are also undoubtedly templates online that you can use for the same.

The next step involves preparing the backing of your wall hanging. You can weave it or use a rug canvas backing and latch hooking techniques. Once you're ready, you need to measure out the dimensions of your canvas.

Once the design is done, it is roughly copied onto the canvas although it need not be perfect because it will be covered by the yarn as you hook the design. If you want to angle the wall hanging, all you need to do is trim the canvas to the desired shape.

Once your design is put down, you just need to start hooking your wall hanging.

Once you complete the rug hooking it is time for finishing. This can be done using a dowel that can be bought in a craft store for less than a dollar. You can customize it using paint and the string a length of yarn through a big plastic needle used for plastic canvas. The wall hanging is then stitched to the dowel by stringing the yarn around the dowel and then through the top layer of the wall hanging. The three pieces are then braided together and the hanger stuck on top. Once that's done, all that is left is to hang it up.

Making Latch Hooking Coasters

There are several ways in which hooked coasters can be finished. There is no one way that it must be done; trial and error can work until you perfect the way that works for you. The coasters are hooked on a frame of appropriate size. Once the hooking is done, the next step is to steam the coasters by placing a damp cloth over the hooked pieces and then using an iron to gently blot them down on both sides.

The steam causes the wool to pull itself down and in, at various places and assimilates into a much better-looking design. Once that is done, the coasters are laid top side up on a waxed piece of paper. To stop the linen from unraveling later when it is cut, the edges are tamped down with glue. A brush or a finger can be used to spread the glue along the edges of the coasters. It is best to apply the glue to both sides of the pieces the top first and then the bottom. This is so as to be able to leave a little air gap for drying when they are turned over. A new sheet of waxed paper is used once the coaster is flipped to avoid the possibility of it sticking to the old paper in case glue got on it, or of glue getting on the wool.

Take a time out to do other things so that the glue can dry or a hair dryer can be used for faster drying. After the coasters have dried, they are cut apart and a quarter or half an inch is left around the edges. The cut edges should not be thrown away because they can be repurposed in other craft pieces.

A piece about the size of the coaster plus edge of double-sided heat-activated plastic is then cut using a Heat Bond or other preferred product. This is a cheap, easily found product that is easy to work with which also keeps moisture away from the surface on which the coaster is being used. The Heat Bond is then placed plastic side down on the back of the coaster and heat from a medium iron is applied. It is allowed to cool for a moment before the paper is peeled back and the bottom side of the coaster will now be coated in plastic.

The wool used for the backing is then placed over the plastic side after which the iron is used again to provide heat. Using a damp cloth between the iron and the backing produces a nice steam effect, which facilitates the transfer of heat through the wool backing and results in a tighter bond. The coaster is then allowed to cool.

The next step is to trim away the excess wool around the edges in a very painstaking way that does not touch any of the loops. Pinking shears can be used for this. Once the edges are cut, one can nip the corners to neaten them further. You can leave it like that, with the linen visible from the sides or you can use overstitch binding to make it less primitive looking.

Conclusion

Rug hooking is a fun if time-consuming craft for DIY enthusiasts. The beauty of the rug hooking craft is that it inspires infinite creativity and imagination. With the right mix of colors, textures, and shapes, you can create customized home décor articles that make your house a real home.

No sources used.

Printed in Great Britain
by Amazon